SCIENCE INTERACTIONS

Course 1

GLENCOE
McGraw-Hill

New York, New York   Columbus, Ohio   Woodland Hills, California   Peoria, Illinois

A Glencoe Program

Science Interactions

Student Edition

Teacher Wraparound Edition

Science Discovery Activities: SE

Science Discovery Activities: TE

Teacher Classroom Resources

Laboratory Manual: SE

Laboratory Manual: TAE

Study Guide: SE

Study Guide: TE

Transparency Package

Computer Test Bank

Performance Assessment

Spanish Resources

Science and Technology Videodisc Series

Science and Technology Videodisc Teacher Guide

Integrated Science Videodisc Program

TO THE STUDENT

This Study Guide for *Science Interactions: Course 1* provides you with an easy way to learn science. Each chapter's worksheets closely follow the chapter text and help you understand major concepts and new vocabulary. The chapter's subject matter is well covered as you complete such tasks as fill-in-the-blank, matching, diagrams, tables, and word puzzles.

Complete the Study Guide for each section of a chapter as you finish the text reading assignments. You will find the directions are simple and easy to follow.

Send all inquiries to:
GLENCOE DIVISION
Macmillan/McGraw-Hill
936 Eastwind Drive
Westerville, OH 43081

ISBN 0-02-826757-5

Printed in the United States of America.

5 6 7 8 9   009   03 02 01 00 99

TABLE OF CONTENTS

STUDY GUIDE

A Tour of Your Textbook

1. Using the Contents Overview on pages vi-viii, how many units are in this textbook? _____

   How many chapters are there? _____

2. Using the Table of Contents on pages xix-1, what is the title of Unit 3? _____

   _____

   How many chapters are in Unit 3? _____

3. What is the title of the Investigate! activity on pages 10–11 of the introduction? _____

   _____

4. Each unit begins with a photograph and an activity called "Try It." On what page is the Try It for

   Unit 1? _____

5. What is the main feature of the Chapter Opening photograph for Chapter 1 on page 20?

   _____

6. How many questions are there in the "Did You Ever Wonder?" for Chapter 2 on page 52?

   _____

7. What is the story about in the Chapter 3 opening on page 84? _____

   _____

8. What is the title of the Explore! at the beginning of Chapter 5? _____

   _____

9. What are the section titles in Chapter 6? _____

   _____

10. What is represented by the series of photographs in Figure 7-7 on pages 228–229? _____

    _____

11. What is the first objective for Section 8–1? _____

    _____

12. According to Figure 9-8 on page 288, is the shell of a crab an exoskeleton or endoskeleton?

    _____

STUDY GUIDE

13. What is the topic of the Find Out! on page 318, Chapter 10? _____

_____

14. What is the title of the Investigate! on pages 354–355 of Chapter 11? _____

_____

15. What is the "Problem" for the Investigate on page 388? _____

_____

16. In the Skillbuilder on page 392, what is the source of the data for making a graph?

_____

17. Find the "A Closer Look" on pages 456–457 in Chapter 14. What is the subject of this feature?

_____

18. What are the Key Science Terms for Chapter 15? _____

_____

_____

19. List the titles of the Expand Your View articles in Chapter 16. _____

_____

_____

20. What are the parts of the Chapter Review for Chapter 19? _____

_____

_____

21. On what page is the Unit Review for Unit 5? _____

22. What is the topic of Appendix E? _____

23. What begins on page 652? _____

24. What is the first page of the Glossary? _____

STUDY GUIDE

Chapter **1**

1-1 Viewing Earth

Match each item in Column I with the most appropriate item in Column II. Write the letter for that item in the blank to the left.

Column I	Column II
_____ **1.** landforms	**a.** cover about half of the United States
_____ **2.** Gulf Coastal Plain	**b.** extend from Appalachians to Rockies
_____ **3.** plains	**c.** formed by Colorado River
_____ **4.** Great Plains	**d.** surface features of Earth
_____ **5.** Interior Plains	**e.** empties into Gulf of Mexico
_____ **6.** mountains	**f.** raised areas of flat land
_____ **7.** plateaus	**g.** flat, grassy, dry plains
_____ **8.** Grand Canyon	**h.** lowlands surrounding Gulf of Mexico
_____ **9.** rivers	**i.** cut through all kinds of landforms
_____ **10.** Mississippi River	**j.** high, steep landforms

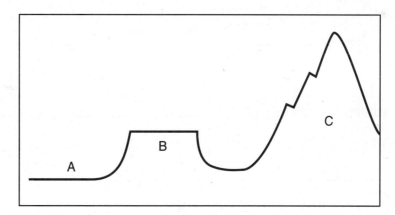

Name each of the major landforms shown at A, B, and C.

A _____   **B** _____   **C** _____

EXPLORE!

How will a cross section profile of the United States help you understand surface features?

_____

_____

STUDY GUIDE
Chapter 1

1-2   Using Maps

In the space provided, write the word or words that best complete(s) the sentence.

1. A way to represent elevation on a flat map is by using _____.

2. Distance in degrees north or south of the equator is called _____.

3. Height above or below sea level is _____.

4. Distance in degrees east or west of the prime meridian is called _____.

5. The difference from one contour line to the next is the contour _____.

Use the following topographical map to answer questions 6–9.

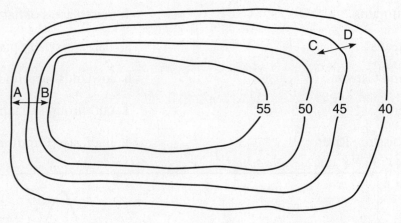

SCALE: 1 cm = 16 m

6. What is the contour interval in the map above? _____

7. Which hike is steeper A to B or C to D? Why? _____

_____

8. Describe the type of landform represented by the map. _____

9. Where would rivers flow faster, A to B or C to D? Why? _____

_____

FIND OUT!
Using the map in the Find Out! activity, how might you direct someone to the airport from

Balmoral Park? _____

_____

STUDY GUIDE

1-3 Viewing the Sky

Fill in the correct words in the sentences.

1. Patterns formed by groups of stars are called _____.

2. Each stage in the cycle of the moon results in the _____ of the moon.

3. The large, dark areas of the moon are called _____.

4. Depressions on the moon caused by meteorites are _____.

5. The location of stars, constellations, and planets are shown on _____ .

6. The sun appears to rise in the _____and set in the _____.

7. In the northern hemisphere, the sun is visible for a _____ length of time in the summer than in the winter.

8. The sun appears to move in the sky because Earth is _____.

9. Many constellations were named for people or _____.

10. Sailors use the constellations for _____.

11. The changing pattern of moonlight visible on Earth repeats every _____days.

EXPLORE!

Using the Explore! activity, you observed the shadows of the sun at several hours in a day. How do

you think people can use these shadows to create a sundial? _____

_____

_____

_____

_____

STUDY GUIDE

Chapter 2

2-1   The Nature of Light

If an object below is a source of light, put the word "source" in the blank. If it reflects light, put the word "reflect."

_____ **1.** match flame

_____ **2.** stars

_____ **3.** unplugged television

_____ **4.** table

_____ **5.** heating element of stove turned on high

Circle the term in the parentheses that correctly completes each sentence.

6. Light travels in (straight, curved) lines.

7. When an object (produces, blocks) light, a shadow is formed.

8. Light can travel from the sun to Earth in about (eight, eighty) minutes.

9. The speed of light is (186 000, 300 000) kilometers per second.

10. The speed of light is (faster, slower) than the speed of sound.

11. Objects that reflect or absorb light but do not allow light to pass through them are (translucent, opaque).

12. A (transparent, opaque) glass candle holder allows enough light through so you can see clearly what's on the other side of the glass.

EXPLORE!

1. Suppose you are putting on a shadow puppet show. Would it be best to make your puppets from

a translucent, opaque, or transparent material? Why? _____

_____

2. A periscope is a type of tube that helps you see around corners. Could you make one by simply

bending a tube from paper towels? Why? _____

_____

STUDY GUIDE

Chapter 2

2-2   Reflection and Refraction

Place the letter M before a statement that is true for a mirror and the letter F before a statement that is true for crumpled foil. If the statement is true for both mirror and foil, put both M and F.

_____ **1.** The surface reflects light in orderly, straight lines.

_____ **2.** The surface reflects light.

_____ **3.** The surface reflects light in straight lines that go in many directions.

_____ **4.** The surface produces a regular reflection.

_____ **5.** The surface produces a diffuse reflection.

Answer the following questions on the lines provided.

6. Why can't you see yourself in the pages of this book? _____

_____

7. Name three materials that reflect light well enough for you to see yourself in them. _____

_____

8. Describe two things you could do to change the direction of light. _____

_____

9. What is the difference between reflection and refraction? _____

_____

10. Why does light refract? _____

_____

_____

EXPLORE!
Would a teaspoon in a glass of water appear straight? Explain. _____

_____

STUDY GUIDE

Chapter 2

2-3 Color

In the blank at the left, write the letter of the choice that best completes the statement or answers the question.

_____ 1. How many colors are in the spectrum?
    a. five   **b.** six   **c.** seven

_____ 2. A tissue that is sensitive to light and can detect all kinds of colors and shapes is the _____.
    a. retina   **b.** iris   **c.** lens

_____ 3. Rods and cones are the nerve cells that send information to your brain through the _____.
    a. lens   **b.** retina   **c.** optic nerve

_____ 4. The muscles that control the size of the pupil according to the amount of light available is the _____.
    a. lens   **b.** iris   **c.** retina

_____ 5. A red shirt _____.
    a. reflects yellow light   **c.** reflects red light
    b. absorbs red light

_____ 6. Light with a blue filter produces blue light because the filter absorbs _____.
    a. all colors   **c.** all colors but blue
    b. blue color

_____ 7. When you mix all the colors of light, you get _____.
    a. black   **b.** green   **c.** white

_____ 8. In your eyes, which cone does not respond to yellow?
    a. blue   **b.** green   **c.** red

_____ 9. Rods are helpful for _____.
    a. seeing in dim light   **c.** seeing color
    b. helping the work of the cones

_____ 10. Which of these is not a primary pigment?
    a. magenta   **b.** yellow   **c.** blue

_____ 11. What color will you get if you mix the pigments magenta and cyan?
    a. green   **b.** red   **c.** blue

_____ 12. What color will you get if you mix all the pigments together?
    a. white   **b.** black   **c.** green

EXPLORE!

The colors of light passing through a prism are the same as the colors in a rainbow. Name them in order. _____

STUDY GUIDE

Chapter 3

3-1 Sources of Sound

The coil below represents sound moving through air. Answer the following questions by writing the correct number in the space provided.

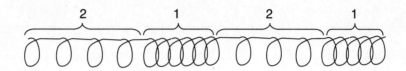

1. Which area of the coil is an area of compression? _____

2. Which area of the coil is an area of rarefaction? _____

3. Which area of the coil represents bunched up air particles? _____

4. Which area of the coil represents spread out air particles? _____

5. Describe how sound travels from an alarm clock to the ear. Include a drawing in your

   explanation. _____

   _____

   _____

   _____

   _____

FIND OUT!

In the Find Out! on page 89, you discovered that sound travels better through a string than through the air. Why do you think sound travels faster through liquids and solids than through gases?

_____

_____

STUDY GUIDE

Chapter 3

3-2 Frequency and Pitch

Listed below are answers. Write a question for each answer. The first one has been done as an example.

1. frequency **What term refers to the number of times an object vibrates in a certain time?**

2. hertz (Hz) _____

3. pitch _____

4. lower pitch _____

5. change the tension _____

6. for feeding and protecting their young _____

FIND OUT!

Use the drawing of the guitar to answer the following questions.

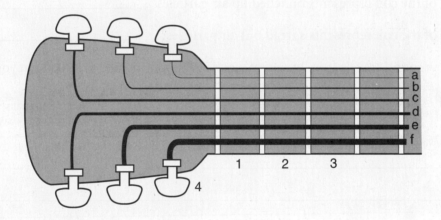

_____ **1.** If all strings are tightened to the same tension, which string will produce the lowest pitch if plucked?

_____ **2.** If all strings are tightened to the same tension, which string will produce the highest pitch if plucked?

_____ **3.** If you pressed on the strings at position 3, would the pitch be higher or lower than the whole string?

_____ **4.** If you turned the key at position 4, making the string tighter, would the pitch of that string be higher or lower?

_____ **5.** If you pressed on the strings at position 1, would the pitch of the strings be higher or lower than at position 3?

STUDY GUIDE

3-3 Music and Resonance

Find the word to complete the following statements and fill in the puzzle to get the complete picture of sound.

1. — — ☐ — —
2. — — ☐ — — —
3. — — — — ☐
4. — ☐ — —
5. — ☐ — —
6. — — — — — ☐ —
7. — — — — — — — —
8. — — ☐ — — — —
9. — — — — — — — —
10. ☐ — — —

1. Because a piano has a different _____ than a guitar, it has a different quality of sound.
2. A sound that tends to be less annoying than noise because it has a pattern is _____.
3. Both music and noise are types of _____.
4. A large guitar will have a different sound quality than a small guitar because of its _____.
5. Sound that tends to be messy and disorganized with no pattern is _____.
6. On a guitar, a _____ vibrates and produces sound.
7. The term that means to resound or sound again is _____.
8. Strumming a guitar will produce a different sound _____ than plucking it.
9. An instrument's _____ affects its sound quality.
10. Resonance occurs when two or more objects vibrate at the _____ frequency.

Fill in the blank below with the term in the black box.

11. Pictures of sound vibrations are _____.

EXPLORE!

How do a tuning fork and a table demonstrate resonance? _____

_____

_____

STUDY GUIDE

Chapter 4

4-1   Composition of Matter

Read each definition. Use words from the chapter to fill in the blanks.

1. __ __ __ __ __ __ __ __ __

2. __ __ __ __ __ __ __ __ __ __ __ __ __

3. __ __ __ __ __ __ __

4. __ __ __ __ __ __ __

5. __ __ __ __ __ __ __ __ __ __ __

6. __ __ __ __ __ __ __ __ __

1. anything that contains only one kind of material
2. mixture in which the different substances are distributed unevenly
3. a substance that cannot be broken down further into simpler substances by ordinary means
4. any material made of two or more substances
5. mixture in which the different substances are distributed evenly throughout
6. a substance whose smallest unit is made up of more than one element

Give an example of each of the following:

7. element _____

8. homogeneous mixture _____

9. heterogeneous mixture _____

FIND OUT!

1. In the Find Out! on the characteristics of water, you observed drops of water under a microscope.

   What can you conclude about each drop of water? _____

   _____

2. In the Find Out! on separating mixtures, you examined a mixture of iron and sulfur. Why would you be able to reproduce this mixture with the same elements once they have been separated?

   _____

   _____

STUDY GUIDE

Chapter 4

4-2 Describing Matter

1. Fill in the following terms in the table below: cm, dm, g, kg, km, mm, 1000 meters, 1/1000 kilogram, 1/1000 meter, 1/100 meter, 1000 grams, 1/10 meter.

Unit	Abbreviation	Size comparison
decimeter		
kilometer		
millimeter		
gram		
kilogram		
centimeter		

2. In the table, which units measure length? _____

3. In the table, which units measure mass? _____

Match the item in Column I with the most appropriate item in Column II. Write the letter for the item in the blank at the left.

Column I

_____ **4.** mass

_____ **5.** density

_____ **6.** length

_____ **7.** volume

Column II

a. amount of space an object or material occupies

b. the distance between two points

c. amount of matter in an object or a material

d. amount of mass an object or material has compared with its volume

8. In Column I, which properties are physical properties? _____

9. In Column I, which properties are used to find density? _____

10. What units of measure are most commonly used to measure the volume of liquids? _____

_____

EXPLORE!

A horse's height is measured in units called hands. A hand is equal to 4 inches. If you were a horse,

how many hands tall would you be? _____ How many centimeters are there in

one hand? _____

STUDY GUIDE
_____ Chapter 4

4-3   Physical and Chemical Changes

If the boldface term makes the sentence true, write "TRUE" in the space provided. If the boldface term makes the sentence false, write the correct word in the space provided.

_____   **1.** When a **physical** change takes place, new substances are formed.

_____   **2.** When a **chemical** change takes place, the makeup of the original substance stays the same.

_____   **3.** A **chemical property** is any characteristic that gives a substance the ability to undergo a chemical change.

_____   **4.** Flammability is an important **physical** property.

_____   **5.** Boiling, melting, and freezing are examples of **physical** changes.

_____   **6.** A chemical property of **water** is light sensitivity.

_____   **7.** In a **physical** change, the physical properties of a substance may change.

_____   **8.** When wood burns, a **chemical** change takes place.

_____   **9. Hydrogen peroxide** may lose its ability to clean wounds if exposed to light.

_____   **10.** A **chemical** change takes place when a log is chopped into splinters.

_____   **11.** Breaking and grinding are examples of **chemical** changes.

_____   **12.** Changes in color, light, smell, or sound are often clues that **physical** changes have taken place.

_____   **13.** The smell of ozone in the air after a thunderstorm is a sign that a **chemical** change has occurred.

FIND OUT!

1. How do changes in physical properties affect substances such as water? _____

_____

_____

2. What changes might you look for that could indicate a chemical change? _____

_____

STUDY GUIDE

Chapter 4

4-4   States of Matter

Use the clues below to complete the puzzle.

Across

3. Water vapor changes to liquid water.

5. It has no definite shape and fills its container.

6. It has a definite volume and changes shape to fit its container.

7. It has a definite shape and volume.

8. This is a mixture of gases.

9. The freezing _____ is reached when a liquid turns to a solid.

Down

1. This speeds up condensation.

2. The process in which a solid becomes a liquid.

4. Liquid water changes to a gas.

10. This is solid water.

Fill in the correct terms above the arrows to complete the diagram below of the three states of matter.

Ice   Liquid water   Water vapor

STUDY GUIDE

Chapter 5

5-1 Types of Solutions

Solve the following crossword puzzle by using the clues provided.

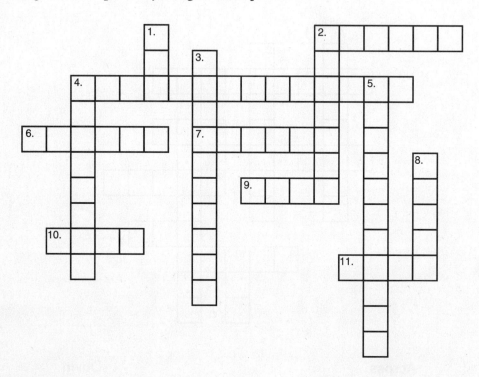

Across

2. the major solute in the ocean or sea is _____ chloride

4. solution of copper and silver (2 words)

6. to mechanically separate a mixture

7. substance that seems to disappear or dissolve in a solvent

9. If you want to increase the rate of solids dissolving in liquids, you apply _____.

10. More gas will stay dissolved in _____ liquid than in warm.

11. When you add sugar to coffee you can _____ the sugar to make it dissolve faster.

Down

1. example of a gas-gas solution

2. substance that does the dissolving

3. solute and solvent becoming evenly mixed

4. mixture that can't be separated by filtering

5. a way to separate the salt from salt water

8. the universal solvent

EXPLORE!

What are some of the properties you discovered in the Explore! on page 156? _____

_____

_____

STUDY GUIDE

5-2   Solubility and Concentration

Graph the data from the table and then answer the questions that follow.

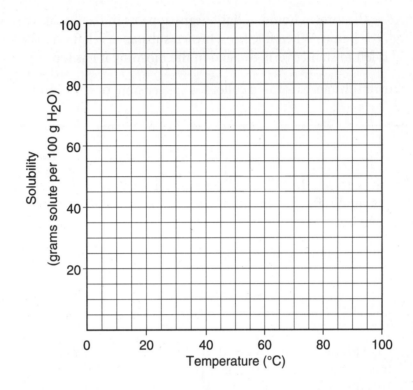

Substance g/100 g water	Temperature (°C)					
	0°	20°	40°	60°	80°	100°
$CuSO_4$	15 g	20 g	30 g	40 g	55 g	79 g
Li_2SO_4	35 g	35 g	33 g	31 g	30 g	29 g
NH_4Cl	30 g	38 g	45 g	55 g	65 g	78 g

_____ **1.** Which substance has the greatest solubility at 0°C?

_____ **2.** Which substance has the greatest solubility at 100°C?

_____ **3.** Which solutions would be saturated at 60°C with 40 g of the substance dissolved in 100 g of water?

_____ **4.** Which substance decreases its solubility as the temperature increases?

_____ **5.** Which solution would be the least saturated at 0°C, with only 2 g of the substance dissolved in 100 g of water?

STUDY GUIDE

5-3 Colloids and Suspensions

Decide whether the following homogenous mixtures are either solutions, colloids, or suspensions, and explain why they fit into that category.

1. You are presented with a brown liquid. A light beam appears in the liquid when you shine a flashlight through the liquid. When filtered, a brown substance is left on the filter paper. The remaining liquid is left to stand overnight, and in the morning it has separated into a clear liquid over a layer of brown substance. Is this a colloid, a suspension, or a solution? Explain.

   _____

   _____

2. Another liquid is given to you. It is blue. A light beam from a flashlight does not appear in the liquid. Some of the liquid is filtered, but nothing remains on the filter paper. Some of the liquid is left to stand overnight but is the same in the morning. You evaporate some of the liquid and blue crystals remain. Is this a colloid, a solution, or a suspension? Explain. _____

   _____

   _____

3. A third liquid you are given is yellow. A beam from a flashlight is seen in the liquid. Some of the liquid is filtered, but nothing is left on the filter paper. Some of the liquid is left to stand overnight but is the same in the morning. You leave some to evaporate, but there is no change in the substance. Is this a solution, a colloid, or a suspension? Explain. _____

   _____

4. How would you proceed to determine whether blood is a colloid, a suspension, or a solution?

   _____

   _____

5. What type of mixture is Italian salad dressing? Describe the properties that support your conclusion. _____

   _____

EXPLORE!

Why do the particles in the muddy water settle to the bottom of the container? _____

_____

STUDY GUIDE

6-1   Properties and Uses of Acids

Match the acids with their uses. Some may be used more than once.

Column I	Column II
_____ **1.** car batteries	**a.** acetic acid
_____ **2.** paper	**b.** ascorbic acid
_____ **3.** pickling	**c.** carbonic acid
_____ **4.** clean concrete or steel	**d.** hydrochloric acid
_____ **5.** vinegar	**e.** sulfuric acid
_____ **6.** carbonated drinks	
_____ **7.** digests food	
_____ **8.** packaged foods	
_____ **9.** fertilizer	
_____ **10.** paint	

Answer the following questions in phrases or complete sentences.

11. What are three properties of acids? _____

12. Why should you never taste an unknown product to see if it is an acid? _____

_____

13. What is it about rain that causes marble structures to crumble? _____

_____

14. If your doctor told you to avoid foods that are acidic, what should you cut from your diet?

_____

15. How have humans affected the natural balance of acids in the environment? _____

_____

_____

FIND OUT!

In a hard water area where lime can build up on a faucet, acids can help to get rid of the lime.

Would you use apple juice or vinegar to clean it? Why? _____

STUDY GUIDE

Chapter 6

6-2 Properties and Uses of Bases

Match the name of the industrial base with its use below. Terms may be used more than once.

Column I	Column II
_____ **1.** drain cleaner	**a.** ammonium hydroxide
_____ **2.** cleans windows	**b.** calcium hydroxide
_____ **3.** oven cleaner	**c.** sodium hydroxide
_____ **4.** used in gardens	
_____ **5.** used to manufacture medicine	
_____ **6.** refrigerants	
_____ **7.** dyes	

Answer the following questions in phrases or complete sentences.

8. Name two similarities that all bases have. _____

9. What word is usually in the chemical name of a base? _____

10. If red litmus paper changes to blue, what does this tell you about the substance? _____

_____

 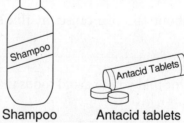 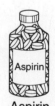

| Vinegar | Oven cleaner | Soap | Shampoo | Antacid tablets | Aspirin |

11. Which items in the above figure may contain bases? _____

_____

FIND OUT!

In the Find Out! activities of this section, you were cautioned not to touch unknown materials.

Why is this important? _____

STUDY GUIDE
Chapter 6

6-3   An Acid or a Base

In the space provided, write the term that best completes the sentence.

1. Food is mixed in the stomach with _____.

2. In the small intestines, food is mixed with _____ from the liver.

3. Blood is a _____ and its pH must be controlled.

Answer the following questions in phrases or complete sentences.

4. Would you rather go swimming in a pool with a pH of 14 or one with a pH of 7?

Explain your answer. _____

5. Is something with a pH of 2 always dangerous to eat? Explain your answer. _____

_____

6. Why do people take antacid tablets? _____

_____

7. Give the change of color in a phenolphthalein strip if dipped into a solution of the following.

lemon _____

ammonia _____

baking soda _____

tomato _____

8. Why must the food nutrients be basic to be used by the body? _____

_____

9. Name some indicators you can use to test for acids and bases. _____

_____

SKILLBUILDER
Why would the pH of rainwater be different from the pH of distilled water? _____

_____

STUDY GUIDE
Chapter 6

6-4   Salts

In the space provided, write the term that best completes the sentence.

1. Mixing lime and acidic soil is an example of _____.

2. Antacids are often taken to neutralize excess _____ in the stomach.

3. When neutralization takes place, a(n) _____ plus water is formed.

4. Another name of table salt is _____.

5. Sodium chloride is the result of a very strong acid and a very strong _____ being mixed together.

6. Table salt has a(n) _____ pH value.

7. An element in household bleach that also may be present in drinking water

    is _____.

8. Limited amounts of _____ are needed to maintain the body's chemical balance.

9. Dr. Lloyd A. Hall developed a technique called _____ for preserving meats.

10. Part of the extinguishing material in one type of fire extinguisher is _____

    _____.

Answer the following questions in the phrases or complete sentences.

11. Why do athletes need to replace salt lost through perspiration? _____

    _____

12. Why do spices need to be sterilized before using them to preserve food? _____

    _____

13. If your doctor told you to cut down on salt you eat, what foods might you cut out of your diet?

    _____

FIND OUT!
If you are mixing ammonia and vinegar together, adding the ammonia drop by drop and then testing the mixture on litmus paper with each addition, what will your first result be? Explain your

answer. _____

STUDY GUIDE

Chapter 7

7-1   What Is the Living World?

In the space provided, write the word from the following list that best describes the statement given:
reproduction, stimulus, adaptation, or response.

_____ **1.** sunflower produces seeds

_____ **2.** unexpected loud noise

_____ **3.** shivering when cold

_____ **4.** wings on a bird

_____ **5.** change in light

_____ **6.** one-celled organism divides

For each organism below, describe how it is adapted to its environment.

 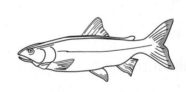 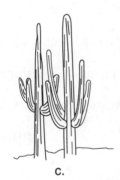

a.   b.   c.

7. a. _____

_____

b. _____

_____

c. _____

_____

FIND OUT!

List two traits of living organisms that you observed in this activity. _____

_____

STUDY GUIDE

Chapter 7

7-2   Classification

Match each item in Column I with the most appropriate item in Column II. Write the letter for that item in the blank to the left. Terms are to be used only once.

Column I		**Column II**
_____ **1.** kingdom that contains organisms that move and are consumers		**a.** mushroom
_____ **2.** divided into groups called orders		**b.** Protists
_____ **3.** member of Protist kingdom		**c.** family
_____ **4.** divided into phyla		**d.** fungi
_____ **5.** member of the Fungus kingdom		**e.** paramecium
_____ **6.** subdivision of an order		**f.** plants
_____ **7.** use light from the sun to make food		**g.** Moneran
_____ **8.** some have one cell, others many cells		**h.** class
_____ **9.** can't move, absorb food from organisms		**i.** kingdom
_____ **10.** one-celled, simple organization		**j.** animal

11. Identify the categories in the classification of the timber wolf.

Classification of the Timber Wolf

_____ **a.** Animal   _____ **e.** Canidae

_____ **b.** Chordata   _____ **f.** Canis

_____ **c.** Mammalia   _____ **g.** *Canis lupus*

_____ **d.** Carnivora

EXPLORE!

How can the choice of scientific names help scientists refer to organisms correctly? _____

_____

_____

STUDY GUIDE

7-3   Modern Classification

If the boldface word makes the sentence true, write "TRUE" in the space provided. If the boldface word makes the sentence false, write the correct term in the space provided.

_____ **1.** Classification helps to show how organisms are **related**.

_____ **2.** Visual traits are **always reliable**.

_____ **3.** **Color and location** are not reliable traits for classification.

_____ **4.** Scientists study **visual traits** to see how organisms are related to those that lived many years ago.

_____ **5.** There are **five** major levels in the classification system scientists use.

_____ **6.** A **dichotomous key** is used to identify organisms.

_____ **7.** Giant pandas are closely related to **bears**.

_____ **8.** Method of reproduction **is not** considered a trait.

_____ **9.** Color, size, and body coverings **can** be used alone to classify animals.

_____ **10.** DNA is a genetic code that **cannot** be used to determine whether or not two organisms are related.

EXPLORE!

List three physical characteristics that the organisms above have in common. Do these traits prove

that these animals are closely related? Explain. _____

_____

_____

STUDY GUIDE _____ Chapter 8

8-1   The Microscopic World

For each item, explain what the terms have in common with one another.

1. *Euglena,* bacteria, paramecium _____

2. soil, air, skin _____

3. growth, digestion, reproduction _____

4. planarian, earthworm, dog _____

5. one-celled organisms, many-celled organisms, viruses _____

   _____

   _____

6. measles, AIDS, rabies _____

7. DNA, protein coat, submicroscopic particles _____

   _____

8. mushroom, bread mold, yeast _____

9. Monera, Protista, Fungi _____

10. rod shape, round, threadlike _____

11. light energy, food, carbon dioxide _____

    _____

EXPLORE!

If you make a microscope slide of dry yeast mixed with warm tap water, what changes might you

observe after 10 minutes? _____

_____

STUDY GUIDE

8-2   Monerans and Protists

In the blank, write the name of the kingdom described.

_____ **1.** all need moist surroundings

_____ **2.** all are one-celled; some use light to make food from water and carbon dioxide

_____ **3.** some are many-celled producers

_____ **4.** none have nuclei

_____ **5.** used in making yogurt and sauerkraut

_____ **6.** bacteria and blue-green bacteria

_____ **7.** *Euglena*, amoeba, algae

Use the diagram below to answer the following questions.

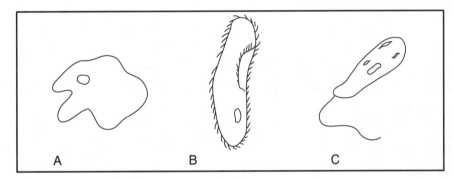

8. Explain the method of movement used by each of the organisms in the figure.

Organism A: _____

Organism B: _____

Organism C: _____

9. Which kingdom do these organisms belong to? _____

10. What characterizes a fourth group of protozoans? Where are they found? _____

_____

EXPLORE!

What is a diatom? _____

_____

_____

STUDY GUIDE

Chapter 8

8-3   Fungus Kingdom

Choose the term from the list below that is best described by each statement. Write the term in the space provided.

parasites	penicillin	spore
yeast	recyclers	bioremediation
threadlike tubes	decompose	biopesticide

1. Using organisms such as soil fungi or bacteria to clean up wastes is called

   _____.

2. The fungi called _____ make bread and pizza crust rise by producing gases.

3. Fungi break down, or _____, organic material.

4. Organisms that live on or in other living things and feed on them are called

   _____.

5. A fungus begins life as a(n) _____.

6. A new kind of cockroach trap that contains a fungus that eats the outer shell of the insect is called

   a(n) _____.

7. One kind of fungus produces _____ that doctors prescribe for patients with diseases caused by certain kinds of bacteria.

8. Fungi are _____ because after they decompose organic materials, they return the materials back to the soil.

9. The body of a fungus is usually a mass of many-celled _____.

EXPLORE!

What information about fungi can be obtained by observing a mushroom? _____

_____

_____

STUDY GUIDE

9-1   What Is an Animal?

Match each item in Column I with the most appropriate item in Column II. Write the letter for that item in the blank to the left.

Column I	Column II
_____ **1.** endoskeleton	**a.** an organism that eats other organisms
_____ **2.** vertebrate	**b.** a skeleton that is within an animal's body
_____ **3.** consumer	**c.** an animal that has a backbone
_____ **4.** exoskeleton	**d.** a system of support outside an animal's body
_____ **5.** invertebrate	**e.** an animal that does not have a backbone

For each item, explain what the terms have in common with one another.

6. crayfish, lobsters, ants _____

_____

7. mouth, liver, stomach _____

_____

8. radial, bilateral _____

_____

9. worms, spiders, jellyfish _____

_____

10. hollow nerve cord, gill slits _____

_____

11. hearing, smell, sight _____

_____

12. need food and water, cannot make own food, move from place to place _____

_____

FIND OUT!
How does a bird's beak affect what it eats? _____

_____

STUDY GUIDE

9-2 Reproduction and Development

Choose the term from the list below that is best described by each statement. Write the term to the left of each statement.

one parent	fertilization	invertebrates	regeneration	external
metamorphosis	internal	vertebrates	incomplete	

_____ **1.** Asexual reproduction is the production of a new organism from _____.

_____ **2.** Change in form is less distinct between stages in _____ metamorphosis.

_____ **3.** When sperm and egg unite, _____ occurs.

_____ **4.** Asexual reproduction occurs in certain _____.

_____ **5.** Lost body parts in some organisms can be replaced by _____.

_____ **6.** An advantage of _____ fertilization is that the animals are not restricted to living in or near water.

_____ **7.** When an organism changes form as it grows from an egg to an adult, _____ has occurred.

8. Identify the labeled stages.

a. _____

b. _____

c. _____

d. _____

e. _____

For each item, explain what the words have in common with one another with regard to reproduction or development.

9. butterflies, fruit flies, grasshoppers _____

_____

10. alligators, chickens, ducks _____

_____

11. smaller number of eggs, don't need to live in water, fertilized eggs are protected from other

animals. _____

STUDY GUIDE

9-3 Adaptations for Survival

Complete the following table with the correct examples or functions of adaptations. Refer to your textbook for help.

Types of adaptations	Examples of adaptations	Functions of adaptations
Body structure	lungs	
	beak	
		used by fish to obtain oxygen for respiration
Behavioral		done by insects to produce sounds that attract mates
	barking or growling	
		allows some animals to blend into their surroundings and hide from enemies

For each item, explain what the terms or phrases have in common.

1. peacock spreading feathers, insects releasing chemicals, insects rubbing their wings _____

_____

2. stripes of a tiger, colors of a chameleon, skin pattern of a copperhead _____

_____

3. gills, openings on the sides of the bodies of insects, lungs _____

_____

4. For each of the labeled bird feet in the figure below, name the function for which it is best adapted.

   a. _____

   b. _____

   c. _____

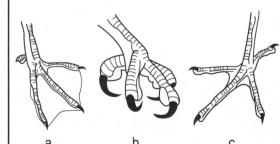

a.   b.   c.

STUDY GUIDE

Chapter 10

10-1 What Is a Plant?

Answer the following questions in phrases or complete sentences.

1. Identify the lettered parts of the diagram, and explain the functions of each part.

a. _____

_____

b. _____

_____

c. _____

_____

2. What are the three traits that separate plants from other living things? _____

_____

_____

In the space provided, write the term from the following list that best completes each statement below.

cuticle	palisade layer	stomata
epidermis	phloem	xylem

_____ **3.** Water, oxygen, and carbon dioxide pass into and out of the leaf through small openings called ____.

_____ **4.** A waxy coating called the ____ protects the plant from dying out.

_____ **5.** The thin layer that covers the upper and lower surfaces of the leaf is called the ____.

_____ **6.** Tubelike vessels that carry water and minerals from the roots through the stem to the leaves make up the ____.

_____ **7.** Most of the food made by leaves is made in the ____.

_____ **8.** Tubelike vessels that move food from the leaves to other parts of the plant make up the ____.

EXPLORE!

Name one characteristic that you share with plants. _____

_____

STUDY GUIDE

──────────────────────────────────── Chapter 10

10-2   Classifying Plants

The characteristics of the three plant groups are listed below. In the space provided, write the name of each group.

1. _____
   - have xylem and phloem
   - have no flowers
   - produce spores

2. _____
   - lack tubelike vessels to transport water, minerals, and food
   - do not have roots, stems, and leaves
   - produce spores

3. _____
   - are largest group of plants on Earth
   - have roots, stems, and leaves
   - produce seeds

Use the names of the three plant groups to answer these questions.

4. Which group do mosses and liverworts belong to? _____

5. Which group do horsetails, club moss, and ferns belong to? _____

6. Which group do gymnosperms and angiosperms belong to? _____

In the space provided, write "G" if the phrase describes a gymnosperm. Write "A" if it describes an angiosperm.

_____ **7.** vascular plant in which the seed is enclosed inside a fruit

_____ **8.** term that means "naked seed"

_____ **9.** flowering plant

_____ **10.** vascular plant that produces seeds on cones

FIND OUT!

In the Find Out! activity, what happened to the celery during the 48 hours it was in the jar? From your observations, determine whether celery is a vascular or nonvascular plant and explain your

answer. _____

_____

_____

STUDY GUIDE

10-3   Plant Reproduction

In the space provided, write the word or phrase that best completes the statement.

1. Nonvascular plants reproduce from _____.

2. Seeds of angiosperms form within a(n) _____.

3. Spores or seeds are produced in _____ reproduction.

4. Seeds of gymnosperms form on _____.

5. Reproduction from roots, stems, or leaves is _____ reproduction.

Match each item in Column I with the most appropriate item in Column II. Write the letter for that item in the blank to the left.

Column I	Column II
_____ **6.** pistil	**a.** swollen base of a pistil
_____ **7.** embryo	**b.** leaflike parts that protect a developing flower
_____ **8.** pollen	**c.** fertilized inside the ovary
_____ **9.** night-blooming flower	**d.** develops within a seed, or a young plant that develops within a seed
_____ **10.** stamen	
_____ **11.** pollination	**e.** has a strong scent that attracts pollinators
_____ **12.** egg	**f.** female reproductive organ
_____ **13.** ovary	**g.** forms in the anther
_____ **14.** sepals	**h.** male reproductive organ
	i. transfer of pollen from the stamen to the stigma

Answer the following question in complete sentences.

15. What are some characteristics of seeds that aid in their dispersal? _____

_____

_____

_____

STUDY GUIDE

Chapter 10

10-4   Plant Processes

Fill in the blanks by answering the questions below. Unscramble the circled letters to complete question 5.

1. __ __ __ O __   O __ __ __ __
2. __ __ __ __ O __ __
3. __ __ __ __ __   __ O O __ __
4. __ __ __ __ O __ __ __ __ __ __ __ __

1. Plants lose large amounts of ____ ____ every day.
2. Water evaporates through openings called ____.
3. The size of the openings through which water evaporates is controlled by ____ ____.
4. Plants lose water vapor through the process of ____.
5. Transpiration takes place in the plant's _____.

Classify each of the terms listed below as a reactant or an end product of photosynthesis.

6. Water: _____

7. Carbon dioxide: _____

8. Sugar: _____

9. Light energy: _____

10. Oxygen: _____

11. Is energy stored or released in photosynthesis? _____

Classify each of the terms listed below as a reactant or an end product of respiration.

12. Carbon dioxide: _____

13. Oxygen: _____

14. Water: _____

15. Sugar: _____

16. Energy: _____

17. Is energy stored or released in respiration? _____

STUDY GUIDE

Chapter 11

11-1   What Is an Ecosystem?

A small pond is a type of ecosystem. Using the figure below, answer the following questions.

1. List the nonliving parts of the

ecosystem. _____

_____

_____

2. List the living parts of the ecosystem.

_____

_____

3. What would be the habitat of a crayfish? _____

_____

4. How could the pond support different species of fish? _____

_____

_____

In the space provided, write the word or phrase from the following list that best matches the statement given: ecosystem, population, habitat, niche, community.

_____ **5.** a frog eating insects on the edge of a pond

_____ **6.** a parrot fish swimming near a coral reef

_____ **7.** a flock of warblers migrating south for the winter

_____ **8.** snakes and owls feeding on field mice

_____ **9.** soil, air, water, and living organisms

FIND OUT!

In the Find Out! you discovered how three species of birds could share the same habitat. Explain

how the different species in the habitat shown on pages 348 and 349 share the habitat. _____

_____

_____

NAME _____ DATE _____ CLASS _____

STUDY GUIDE

Chapter 11

11-2   Organisms in Their Environments

Match each item in Column I with the most appropriate item in Column II. Write the letter for that item in the blank to the left.

	Column I		Column II
_____	**1.** bacteria in soil change this to a form that can be used by plants		**a.** producer
_____	**2.** able to make own food		**b.** consumer
_____	**3.** burning these increases the amount of carbon dioxide in the atmosphere		**c.** decomposer
_____	**4.** all possible feeding relationships in an ecosystem		**d.** energy
_____	**5.** process by which green plants use light energy from the sun to make food		**e.** photosynthesis
_____	**6.** water, elements, and nutrients being used more than once		**f.** food chain
_____	**7.** increases species' chances of survival		**g.** food web
_____	**8.** passed from organism to organism in food		**h.** recycling
_____	**9.** mold and mushrooms are members of this kingdom		**i.** varied diet
_____	**10.** parts include evaporation, clouds, and rain		**j.** water cycle
_____	**11.** organism that gets food by breaking down dead organisms into nutrients		**k.** nitrogen
_____	**12.** a single line of interactions that show energy transfer in an ecosystem		**l.** protein
_____	**13.** one gas is used for respiration and the waste product is used for photosynthesis		**m.** fungus
_____	**14.** nitrogen is used by most organisms to make this product		**n.** fossil fuels
_____	**15.** cannot make its own food		**o.** oxygen-carbon dioxide cycle

EXPLORE!

Give three examples of producers and three examples of consumers not listed in the Explore! Activity.

_____

_____

_____

Copyright © Glencoe Division of Macmillan/McGraw-Hill

41

STUDY GUIDE

Chapter 11

11-3 How Limiting Factors Affect Organisms

Match each item in Column I with the most appropriate item in Column II. Write the letter for that item in the blank to the left. Answers will be used more than once.

Column I	Column II
_____ **1.** predator	**a.** adaptation
_____ **2.** rainfall	**b.** living limiting factor
_____ **3.** increased number of red blood cells	**c.** nonliving limiting factor
_____ **4.** drought	
_____ **5.** temperature	
_____ **6.** prey	
_____ **7.** pollution	
_____ **8.** thick wool coats of alpacas	
_____ **9.** humans	
_____ **10.** blood that freezes at very low temperature	
_____ **11.** competition	
_____ **12.** nutrients in soil	
_____ **13.** spine-like leaves of cactus	
_____ **14.** population size	
_____ **15.** sunlight	

In the space provided, write the word or term that best completes the sentence.

16. Animals that catch and eat other animals are called _____.

17. Any condition that influences the growth or survival of an organism is a(n)

_____.

18. When two organisms try to fill the same niche, _____ results.

19. A limiting factor at ground level in a rainforest is _____.

20. The success of an organism within its environment depends on how well it is

_____ to that environment.

STUDY GUIDE

Chapter 12

12-1   Position, Distance, and Speed

Refer to the figure to answer questions 1-2.

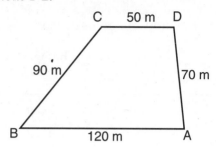

1. What is the total distance that John travels if he goes from A to B to C to D and back again to A?

_____

2. If John covers the distance in 2 minutes, what is his average speed in meters per minute?

_____

Match each item in Column I with the most appropriate item in Column II. Write the letter for that item in the blank to the left.

Column I	Column II
_____ **3.** position	**a.** rate of motion at any given time
_____ **4.** seconds	**b.** location
_____ **5.** reference point	**c.** distance traveled divided by a time interval
_____ **6.** distance	**d.** change in position
_____ **7.** meter	**e.** how far you travel along a path
_____ **8.** instantaneous speed	**f.** S.I. unit for measuring distance
_____ **9.** speed	**g.** used to determine position
_____ **10.** motion	**h.** S.I. unit for measuring time

EXPLORE!

Suppose you have two kinds of graph paper. One kind has squares that are 1 cm on each side. The other kind has squares that are 1/2 cm on each side. Which kind of paper would make it easier for

you to describe the location of a dot to someone else? Why? _____

_____

_____

STUDY GUIDE

Chapter 12

12-2   Velocity

Answer the following questions in phrases or complete sentences.

1. Joyce walks 2 km to a friend's home, stops for an hour to visit, then returns home. What is the

total distance she travels? _____ What was the total displacement? Why?

_____

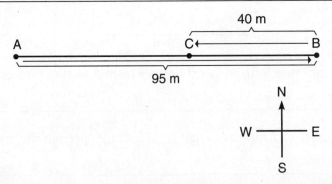

2. Suppose you walked 95 meters east from point A to point B in the figure above, then turned

around and walked 40 meters west to point C. What distance did you walk? _____

3. What is the total displacement for question 2? _____

*The information in two of the phrases is true for that term. Write the letters of the true phrases in the
blank to the left.*

_____ **4.** displacement
   a. net change in position of an object
   b. describe by length and direction
   c. includes speed and direction

_____ **5.** relative velocity
   a. determined from the frame of reference of another object
   b. is always the same
   c. both objects may be moving

_____ **6.** average velocity
   a. measured in m/s^2
   b. includes direction
   c. total displacement divided by total time

EXPLORE!

How will the velocity of the car relative to the paper change if the paper is not moved?

_____

STUDY GUIDE

12-3 Acceleration

If the boldface word makes the sentence true, write "TRUE" in the space provided. If the boldface word makes the sentence false, write the correct term in the space provided.

_____ **1. Velocity** involves both speed and direction.

_____ **2.** Acceleration is the rate at which one's **speed** is changing.

_____ **3.** Acceleration at each instant is called **average** acceleration.

_____ **4. Average acceleration** is the change in velocity divided by the time interval during which the change occurs.

_____ **5.** Zero acceleration indicates zero change in **position.**

Answer the following questions in phrases or complete sentences.

6. Suppose you are on a bobsled and speeding up as you move. If your speed changes by 3 meters per second for every second that you move, what is your acceleration? _____

7. If a toy car speeds up from 0 to 16 meters/second in 12 seconds, what is the car's average acceleration? _____

8. If a car speeds up from 0 to 40 meters/second in 10 seconds, what is the car's average acceleration?

_____

9. How is instantaneous acceleration different from average acceleration? _____

_____

_____

10. Imagine that you are on a sled whose velocity is changing uniformly. Your velocity is 4 m/s at 15 s into the run and 6 m/s at 16 s into the run. What is your acceleration in that second?

_____

11. If you calculate your acceleration relative to a stationary object and then an object moving with uniform velocity, the value would be the same. Explain. _____

_____

_____

STUDY GUIDE

12-4   Motion Along Curves

Use the figure to answer questions 1-2.

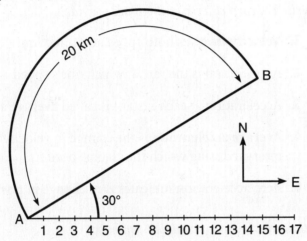

1. What is the distance from A to B along the curve? _____

2. What is the displacement from A to B? _____

In the space provided, write the term that best completes the sentence.

3. The direction of the acceleration of an object moving at a constant speed along a circular path is

   toward the center of the circle. This acceleration is called _____.

4. A device that shows acceleration inward when moving in a circle is a(n)

   _____.

5. Centripetal acceleration is directed toward the _____ of a circular path.

6. To calculate average velocity, you need time of travel and _____.

7. The actual distance traveled along a curved path will be greater than the _____.

8. Acceleration, as in a tilt-a-whirl, occurs because of a change in both speed and

   _____.

9. As an elevator moves upward, a person on the elevator feels pushed _____.

EXPLORE!
How can the bubble accelerometer be used to prove that, along a circular path, acceleration is

toward the center of the circle? _____

_____

STUDY GUIDE

Chapter 13

13-1   Falling Bodies

From the windows of the apartment building pictured, two students, after blocking off the sidewalk so no one would be injured, conducted experiments about falling objects. Answer the following questions regarding these experiments in the spaces provided.

1. Juan dropped a 5-kg pumpkin from apartment A at the same time Janine dropped a 1/2-kg grapefruit from apartment B. Would one reach the sidewalk first? If so, which one? _____

_____

2. Juan dropped a 5-kg pumpkin from apartment F at the same time Janine dropped a similar 5-kg pumpkin from apartment B. Which one was travelling faster when it reached the sidewalk? _____

_____

3. Juan dropped a 5-kg pumpkin from apartment H, and it took 2 seconds to reach the sidewalk. What was its final velocity when it hit the sidewalk? _____

4. If Janine drops a 5-kg pumpkin from apartment A and Juan drops a 5-kg pumpkin from apartment H, will the acceleration due to gravity be different? _____

_____

5. If this apartment building were on the moon and Juan dropped a basketball from apartment F, what would be the final velocity when it hits the moon's surface after 10 seconds? (The acceleration of gravity on the moon is about 1.6 m/s^2.)

_____

FIND OUT!

You can be a human pendulum bob on the end of a rope swing, dropping from a pre-set height. Will you fall more quickly with or without a 20-kg weight attached to your ankles?

_____

STUDY GUIDE
_____ Chapter 13

13-2   Projectile Motion

In the space provided, write the term from the following list that best completes the statement. Answers may be used more than once.

constant	horizontal	projectile
independent	vertical	

1. A rock thrown in the air is a(n)_____.

2. A baseball thrown from one player to another has both _____ and vertical motion.

3. A fork dropped in the kitchen has _____ motion.

4. The part of motion that moves across the ground is called the _____ component.

5. The part of motion that moves down toward Earth is called the _____ component.

6. Vertical and horizontal components are _____ of each other.

7. The horizontal component has a(n) _____ velocity.

8. The _____ component has an acceleration of 9.8 m/s^2.

Circle the term in parentheses that best completes each statement.

9. A ball thrown upward at an angle (speeds up, slows down, maintains the same velocity) in the horizontal direction.

10. The vertical and horizontal components of (projectiles fired horizontally, all projectiles) are independent.

11. The horizontal component of a projectile's motion has (constant velocity, acceleration equal to g).

12. The vertical component of a projectile's motion has (constant velocity, acceleration equal to g).

FIND OUT!
If dropped from the same height, will a coin dropped straight down reach the floor sooner than one

with a forward motion? Explain your answer. _____

_____

STUDY GUIDE

Chapter 13

13-3   Circular Orbits of Satellites

Solve the puzzle below by writing the term in the diagram that best completes each statement. Spelled vertically in the black box you will find one kind of satellite.

1. __ __ ☐ __ __ __ __ __ __ __ __ __ __ __

2. ☐ __ __ __ __ __

3. ☐ __ __ __ __ __

4. ☐ __ __ __ __

5. __ ☐ __ __ __ __

6. ☐ __ __ __

7. __ __ __ ☐ __ __

8. ☐ __ __ __ __ __

9. __ __ __ ☐ __ __ __ __ __

10. __ __ __ ☐ __ __ __ __ __ __ __

11. __ __ __ __ ☐ __ __

12. ☐ __ __ __

13. __ __ __ __ ☐ __ __

1. As you travel farther from Earth, ____ due to gravity decreases.
2. The space shuttle in ____ around Earth is in free-fall.
3. All body functions are carefully ____ during a space flight.
4. Newton was one of the first scientists to describe projectile ____.
5. If a projectile's fall matches Earth's ____ , the projectile will not hit Earth.
6. Satellite motion was predicted by ____.
7. Relative to a person on Earth, a satellite that orbits once a day would appear to not be ____.
8. One effect of weightlessness is the loss of ____ in the bones.
9. A satellite that appears to be motionless is called a(n) ____ satellite.
10. Acceleration toward Earth in free-fall is ____.
11. Satellites orbiting Earth never escape its ____.
12. A stationary satellite orbits Earth ____ each day.
13. The first artificial satellite launched into orbit was ____.

STUDY GUIDE

13-4   The Motion of a Pendulum

Identify whether each statement describes period, frequency, or amplitude. Write the correct term in the space provided.

_____ **1.** A pendulum on a grandfather clock swings back and forth once in 1/4 second.

_____ **2.** A circus performer on a trapeze travels 15 meters from the release point to the lowest point.

_____ **3.** A yo-yo swings from your hand two times in one second.

_____ **4.** A tether ball attached to the ceiling of your basement travels 37 cm after being hit.

_____ **5.** A child in a swing swings back and forth once every ten seconds.

Circle the correct answer in each statement.

6. The (mass of a bob, length of the pendulum) will affect the period of the pendulum.

7. Hertz is used for (frequency, amplitude).

8. When you perform scientific experiments, the factors you test are called (variables, constants).

9. During an experiment, the factor that is changed by the value of the other variables is called the (independent, dependent) variable.

10. Oscillations are (single, back and forth) motions.

Study the pictures below and answer the following questions.

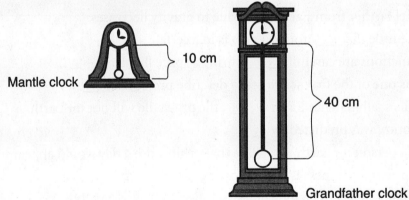

11. If both clocks have an amplitude of 10 cm, which clock will have the longer period? _____

_____

12. The grandfather clock pendulum swings back and forth once every second. What is its

frequency? _____

STUDY GUIDE

14-1   Water Recycling

The information in two of the phrases following each term is true for that term. The information in the other phrase is not true for that term. In the space provided, place the letters of the two statements that are true.

_____ **1.** Evaporation
  a. can be increased by direct sun.   **c.** causes water to change to water vapor.
  b. involves only water from the ocean.

_____ **2.** Condensation
  a. changes water vapor to liquid water.   **c.** involves heat from the sun.
  b. causes clouds to form.

_____ **3.** Precipitation
  a. consists of rain, snow, and hail.
  b. occurs when water droplets float in the air.
  c. occurs when water droplets become too heavy for clouds to hold.

_____ **4.** Hydrologic cycle
  a. is how water is recycled on Earth.
  b. consists of erosion, condensation, flooding, and meanders.
  c. uses the sun for heat.

_____ **5.** Evaporation
  a. is demonstrated when the water level of a glass of water lowers over a period of time.
  b. is demonstrated by the disappearance of a puddle of water.
  c. is demonstrated by rainfall.

SKILLBUILDER

Use the following terms to label the stages in the hydrologic cycle: evaporation, condensation, precipitation.

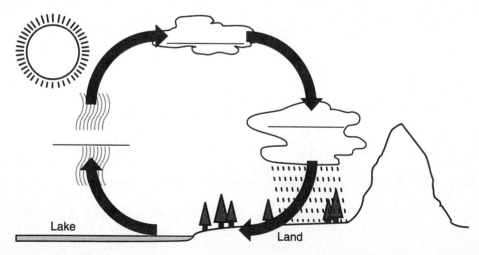

Lake   Land

STUDY GUIDE

Chapter 14

14-2   Streams and Rivers

Answer each question in complete sentences.

1. As rain begins to fall on Earth, trace how a drainage system is formed. _____

_____

_____

_____

2. What area of the United States is drained by the Mississippi River? Include other rivers and where

the Mississippi empties. _____

_____

_____

_____

Below are diagrams of three types of rivers. Describe the features of the rivers and the slope of the land found there.

a.   b.   c.

a. _____

_____

b. _____

_____

c. _____

_____

STUDY GUIDE

14-3   Groundwater in Action

Answer the following questions in the spaces provided.

1. Rocks that do not allow water to pass through are _____.

2. Air spaces in rock and soil are called _____.

3. A permeable layer of sand, gravel, or rock can be a(n) _____.

4. A material in soil that water soaks into quickly is _____.

5. A rock that can be porous and permeable is _____.

6. A soil type that is impermeable is _____.

7. A rock that allows water to pass through it is said to be _____.

8. An aquifer is like a(n) _____ but drains water underground.

Describe a, b, c, and d in the diagram below.

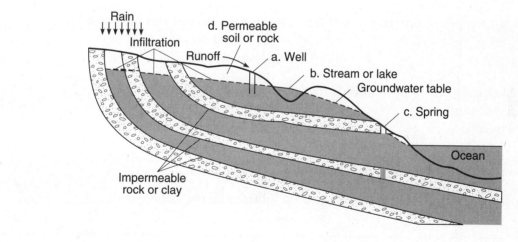

a. _____

_____

b. _____

_____

c. _____

_____

d. _____

_____

STUDY GUIDE

15-1   Gravity

In the blank at the left, write the letter of the choice that best completes the statement.

_____ **1.** The process by which a stream dumps sediment is called _____.
     a. erosion   **c.** a rockslide
     b. deposition   **d.** slump

_____ **2.** When soil moves down a hill, it is called _____.
     a. erosion   **c.** a rockslide
     b. deposition   **d.** a mudslide

_____ **3.** A slow movement of soil down a hill, causing trees to lean, is called _____.
     a. slump   **c.** creep
     b. a mudflow   **d.** a rockslide

_____ **4.** When the weight of the soil on top is too much to be supported by the soil underneath and a mass of soil slips down the slope, it is called _____.
     a. slump   **c.** a rockslide
     b. creep   **d.** a mudflow

_____ **5.** If you see a pile of broken rocks at the bottom of a cliff, you should watch for _____.
     a. slump   **c.** mudflows
     b. creep   **d.** rockslides

_____ **6.** After a heavy rain, a steep hillside made of loose dirt may experience _____.
     a. deposition   **c.** creep
     b. a mudflow   **d.** a rockslide

Answer the following questions in complete sentences.

7. Why are people who build their homes on steep hillsides taking a chance? _____

_____

8. Why are steep banks left when roadways are cut through land sometimes covered with concrete?

_____

9. Why would you especially notice areas where there is creep in the northern climates?

_____

_____

EXPLORE!

Name three ways nature causes erosion. _____

STUDY GUIDE

Chapter 15

15-2   Running Water

Use the figure to answer the questions below.

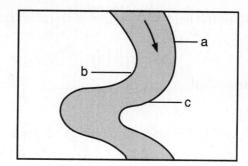

1. At which point in the river will the most erosion occur? _____

2. How will the speed of the meandering stream compare with a stream flowing down a steep hill?

_____

3. What will happen to the valley if the river continues to meander through it? _____

_____

Answer the following questions in complete sentences.

4. How does the rate of flow of a stream affect the amount of sediment it can carry? _____

_____

5. When sediment begins to settle out of flowing water, what part settles out first? _____

_____

6. Explain how swiftly flowing rivers create sediment. _____

_____

7. Would a delta be a fertile area for growing plants? Explain your answer. _____

_____

8. What can you infer about the speed of a stream of water if the valley through which it is flowing

has very steep sides? _____

EXPLORE!

What causes river water to be brownish in color after a heavy rain? _____

_____

STUDY GUIDE
_____ Chapter 15

15-3 Glaciers

In the space provided, write the term that best completes the sentence.

1. A period of time when most of the land was covered with ice and snow is known as a(n)

   _____.

2. Large masses of ice and snow called _____ still cover about one-tenth of Earth's surface.

3. As snow piles up and doesn't melt, it becomes so heavy that the bottom layer turns to

   _____.

4. Masses of ice and snow that cover Greenland and Antarctica are called

   _____ glaciers.

5. Glaciers formed in high mountains are called _____ glaciers.

6. At one time, _____ glaciers covered part of the United States.

7. Glaciers push _____ in front of them.

8. Most of Earth's fresh water is stored in _____.

Answer the questions below in complete sentences.

9. Explain how glaciers form sediment. _____

   _____

10. If there is a shortage of fresh water in the world in the future, what is a possible solution?

    _____

11. Explain what causes a glacier to move. _____

    _____

    _____

FIND OUT!
How do things as hard as rocks get grooves from glaciers? _____

_____

STUDY GUIDE
Chapter 15

15-4   Wind Erosion

In the space provided, write the term that best completes the sentence.

1. During the late 1930s, the Central Plains in the United States became so dry it was called the

   _____.

2. Sand, clay, silt, and other loose sediments can be moved by _____.

3. The cycle of change that constantly shapes the land around you includes

   _____ and deposition.

4. The shapes of _____ are always changing.

5. Sand dunes are formed by the _____ of sand.

6. Once sand dunes are formed, they are continuously _____.

Answer the following questions in complete sentences.

7. Along some beaches it is illegal to remove beach grasses. Why do you think this is so?

   _____

8. Why are dunes along oceans important? _____

   _____

9. Egypt has many ancient structures. How has the desert changed them? _____

   _____

10. How can farmers keep their soil from blowing away? _____

    _____

11. What do you think will happen to the fertility of a farmer's field if the wind blows the topsoil

    away? _____

FIND OUT!
If a dune was in a location that had a wind coming from the west, which side of the dune would be

the steepest? _____

STUDY GUIDE

Chapter 16

16-1   Succession—Building New Communities

In each of the following statements, a word or phrase has been scrambled. Unscramble the word or phrase and write it on the correct line in the puzzle.

1. When one community is slowly replaced by another, the process of change is called **cceusisosn.**

2. As an environment changes, new **sonoictidn** make it possible for other species to grow, reproduce, and increase in number.

3. The first species to live in a new ecosystem are **niepoer** species.

4. Climax communities do not remain **dunsitbrued** forever.

5. The gophers of Mount Saint Helens are an example of one species affecting the **coveryre** of a whole ecosystem.

6. Diversity is the presence of many different **cepseis** within a community.

7. A change in plant **oltupniopa** usually results in a change in the number of animals in an ecosystem.

8. Organisms made up of algae and fungi living together are called **heclnis.**

9. In a **licaxm ommucnyit,** the plant and animal species living there are well adapted to the present conditions.

10. Succession and the recovery of ecosystems depends on **eridsyitv.**

1. _ _ _ _ | _ _ _ _ _ _
2.   _ _ _ _ _ _ _ _ _ _
3.   _ _ _ | _ _ _ _
4.   _ _ _ | _ _ _ _
5. _ _ _ _ _ _ _ _ _
6.   _ _ | _ _ _ _
7. _ _ _ _ _ | _ _ _ _
8.   _ _ _ | _ _ _
9.   _ _ _ | _ _ _ _ _ _ _
10.   _ _ _ _ _ | _ _ _

EXPLORE!

Fill in the blank with the term in the box.

In the Explore! you learned that _____ can be transformed.

STUDY GUIDE

16-2 Interactions in an Ecosystem

Identify the type of symbiotic relationship described in each statement using the following terms:
mutualism, commensalism, and parasitism.

_____ **1.** the pea crab eating tiny organisms that would harm mussel shells

_____ **2.** an African honey guide bird attracting a honey badger's attention

_____ **3.** mistletoe sucking sap from a tree

_____ **4.** orchids living in a tree

_____ **5.** a remora fish attaching itself to a shark

_____ **6.** a mosquito sucking blood from an animal

_____ **7.** the cleaner wrasse eating organisms living on coral cod

_____ **8.** Spanish moss living on a tropical tree in South America

Answer the following questions in complete sentences.

9. What is a symbiotic relationship? _____

_____

10. Why do species compete in an ecosystem? _____

_____

11. Explain how a growing pine tree affects the environment. _____

_____

EXPLORE!

In the Explore! on page 521, you researched ways people change the environment to make it more suitable for themselves. In the 1930s and 1940s people made the prairie more suitable for them by killing prairie dogs. Describe one alternative that could have been taken to reduce the number of

prairie dogs. _____

_____

_____

STUDY GUIDE

Chapter 16

16-3   Extinction—A Natural Process

Answer the following questions in complete sentences and fill in the table.

1. What is extinction? _____

2. What is one possible cause of extinction? _____

   _____

3. What is the difference between local extinction and global extinction? _____

   _____

   _____

4. Name three ways humans can cause extinction. _____

   _____

   _____

5. Identify two ways nations can help save the environment. _____

   _____

   _____

   _____

6. Identify several ways you as an individual can help save the environment. _____

   _____

   _____

   _____

7. Complete the table to show the five mass extinctions on Earth.

Mass extinction	Years ago	Species affected
First		most sea species
Second	370 million	
Third	225 million	
Fourth		75 percent of sea-dwelling species and some land species
Fifth		

STUDY GUIDE

Chapter 17

17-1   Waves and Vibrations

Label the diagrams in the spaces provided, using the following terms.

transverse wave	compression
longitudinal wave	rarefactions

Wave movement

Disturbance

Wave movement

Disturbance

_____ _____

_____   _____

1. On each of the wave diagrams above, use arrows to show:
   a. the direction of wave movement
   b. the direction of medium disturbance

Answer the following questions in phrases or complete sentences.

2. What kind of wave vibrates in the same direction as it travels? _____

3. What kind of wave travels through matter? _____

4. What is the matter through which a wave moves? _____

5. What are the names for the bunching up and spreading out of air that carries a sound wave?

_____

6. What kind of wave travels at right angles to the direction of the disturbance? _____

_____

7. What kind of wave is produced by earthquakes? _____

FIND OUT!

What is the purpose of the open-ended can on the radio speaker in the Find Out! on page 543?

_____

_____

STUDY GUIDE

17-2 Wave Characteristics

Use the diagram to identify the characteristics of a transverse wave. Write the letter of each part on the line provided.

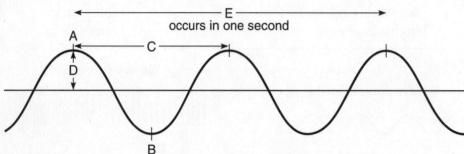

_____ **1.** frequency

_____ **2.** crest

_____ **3.** amplitude

_____ **4.** wavelength

_____ **5.** trough

Describe the relationship between the following terms in the space provided.

6. crest, trough _____

_____

7. wavelength, frequency _____

_____

8. speed, medium _____

_____

SKILLBUILDER

From what you know about how sound travels, would you predict that sound travels faster through

aluminum than through milk? _____

_____

STUDY GUIDE

17-3 Adding Waves

The information in two of the phrases following each term is true for that term. The information in the other phrase is not true for that term. Write the letters of the true phrases in the blank at the left.

_____ **1.** loud noises
  a. can damage the human eardrum
  b. can result in permanent loss of hearing
  c. cannot be muffled by ear protection

_____ **2.** ear protector
  a. absorbs noises
  b. normal conversation cannot be heard
  c. reflects noises

_____ **3.** interference
  a. waves bounce off other waves
  b. emerge on the other side unchanged
  c. two waves can exist in the same place

_____ **4.** constructive interference
  a. two or more waves added together
  b. adding a crest and trough
  c. the new wave is the sum of the amplitudes

_____ **5.** destructive interference
  a. the addition of a crest and trough
  b. can cause a smooth area in wavy water
  c. the new wave is larger than each original wave

Answer the following question in complete sentences in an organized paragraph.

6. Explain how destructive interference can protect human hearing. _____

_____

_____

_____

FIND OUT!

Describe how crests and troughs appear on a white sheet of paper at the bottom of a dish filled with

water. _____

_____

STUDY GUIDE

17-4   Sounds as Waves

Choose the term from the list below that is best described by each statement. Write the term to the left of each statement.

longitudinal wave	frequency	radar
Doppler effect	wavelength	pitch
hearing loss	amplitude	

_____ **1.** the loudness of sound

_____ **2.** used in detecting speeding motorists

_____ **3.** the number of compressions of a sound wave that pass by a certain point each second

_____ **4.** sound wave

_____ **5.** distance from one compression to the next compression

_____ **6.** can be caused by excessive exposure to either high or low frequency sound waves

_____ **7.** a change in frequency due to a moving sound source or moving receiver

_____ **8.** how the ear recognizes frequency

In the space provided, answer the following questions in complete sentences.

9. Explain how sound can damage your hearing. _____

_____

_____

_____

10. Explain the change in pitch of a car horn as it moves by you. _____

_____

_____

FIND OUT!

Explain how you were able to "see" sound in the Find Out! activity. _____

_____

_____

STUDY GUIDE

Chapter 18

18-1   Earthquakes, Volcanoes, and You

Solve the puzzle below by writing the term in the diagram that best completes each statement. You will find another term spelled vertically in the black box.

1. __ __ __ __
2. __ __ __ __ __ __
3. __ __ __ __ __
4. __ __ __ __ __ __ __ __ __ __
5. __ __ __ __ __
6. __ __ __ __ __ __ __
7. __ __ __ __ __ __ __ __ __
8. __ __ __ __ __ __ __ __
9. __ __ __ __ __ __
10. __ __ __ __ __

1. Magma that reaches Earth's surface is called ____.
2. An earthquake occurs when part of the solid Earth below the surface suddenly ____.
3. Large lumps of lava are called ____.
4. The sudden shifting of earth causing rocks and soil to vibrate is called a(n) ____.
5. Molten material beneath the surface on Earth is called ____.
6. Any time volcanic material reaches Earth's surface, it is considered a(n) ____.
7. As you travel toward the interior of Earth, the temperature ____.
8. One direction of movement of buildings from earthquake vibrations is ____.
9. All ____ originate when melted rock rises to the surface of Earth.
10. During an earthquake, ____ travel out in all directions from the spot of origin.

Fill in the blank below with the term in the black box.

11. Earthquakes can occur when _____ move through Earth like waves.

FIND OUT!

What types of volcanoes are represented by the plaster of paris model and the sand or sugar model?

_____

_____

STUDY GUIDE _____ Chapter 18

18-2 Earthquake and Volcano Destruction

If the boldface term makes the sentence true, write "TRUE" in the space provided. If the boldface term makes the sentence false, write the correct term in the space provided.

_____ **1.** Most **earthquakes** are so weak that people don't notice them.

_____ **2.** The **closer** the origin of an earthquake to an inhabited area, the greater the destruction.

_____ **3.** Earthquakes vibrate **loosely packed sediments,** causing structures to collapse.

_____ **4.** Fire is a hazard because natural gas lines are often split open by an earthquake, and sparks may ignite the **escaping gas.**

_____ **5.** A huge, rapidly moving water wave, caused by an earthquake under the ocean floor, is called a **volcano.**

_____ **6.** **Volcanic dust** can block sunlight, which can lower temperature and affect weather.

_____ **7.** Currently, **less than 600** volcanoes on Earth are classified as active.

_____ **8.** Herculaneum and **Venice** were the two cities that were buried by the eruption of Mount Vesuvius in the year 79.

_____ **9.** **Mount Tambora** violently erupted, releasing 6 million times more energy than an atomic bomb.

_____ **10.** Currently, the most active volcano in the world is **Mount Saint Helens.**

_____ **11.** Tsunamis can travel at speeds of more than **700** kilometers per hour.

_____ **12.** A tsunami wave will get taller as the wave reaches **deeper** water.

EXPLORE!

1. In the Explore! activity, what is represented by pounding on the underside of the pan?

_____

2. Does hitting the pan cause all the sand in the pan to move or just the sand directly over the area

that is being pounded? _____

_____

STUDY GUIDE

Chapter 18

18-3   Measuring Earthquakes

Match each item in Column I with the most appropriate item in Column II. Write the letter for that item in the blank to the left.

Column I	Column II
_____ 1. earthquake	**a.** developed to describe the strength of an earthquake
_____ 2. seismologist	**b.** records earthquake vibrations
_____ 3. magnitude	**c.** caused by shifting rock deep in Earth
_____ 4. Richter scale	**d.** earthquake measurement with the most energy
_____ 5. seismograph	**e.** measurement of the strength of an earthquake
_____ 6. 4.0 Richter scale	**f.** most common magnitude of earthquakes
_____ 7. 8.0 Richter scale	**g.** 6200 earthquakes expected a year at this magnitude
_____ 8. 1.0–3.9 Richter scale	**h.** scientist who studies earthquakes

Answer the following questions in complete sentences.

9. In a seismograph, why does the pen have to be freely moving? _____

_____

_____

10. What does each number on the Richter scale represent and how do they compare to each other?

_____

_____

SKILLBUILDER

Using Table 18-2 on page 592 of your textbook as a reference, make a table to show three strong earthquakes recorded in the United States.

Year	Location	Richter value	Deaths

STUDY GUIDE

— Chapter 19

19-1   Earth's Shape and Movements

Fill in the following table with information about each of the equinoxes and solstices.

	Date of occurrence	Season starting in Northern Hemisphere	Season starting in Southern Hemisphere	Position of sun
Equinox	September 22			directly over the equator
Solstice		winter		Tropic of Capricorn
Equinox			fall	
Solstice				Tropic of Cancer

Circle the word or words that correctly complete each statement.

1. The (tilt, revolution) of Earth causes the change in seasons.

2. Earth's path around the sun is in the shape of a(n) (circle, ellipse).

3. Earth is farthest from the sun in (July, January) and closest to the sun in (July, January).

4. The half of Earth tilting toward the sun receives sunlight for (fewer, more) hours each day.

5. Earth is (sphere, circle) -shaped, but bulges slightly at the equator and is somewhat flattened at the poles.

6. Earth rotates once every 24 hours around an imaginary line, called Earth's (axis, poles).

7. A complete (rotation, revolution) around the sun takes about 365 1/4 days.

8. When the sun reaches a(n) (equinox, solstice), night and day are the same length all over the world.

FIND OUT!

How does the Find Out! explain the effect of the shape of Earth on the horizon as sailors approach

land? _____

_____

_____

_____

STUDY GUIDE

Chapter 19

19-2   Motions of the Moon

Use the figure below to answer the following questions.

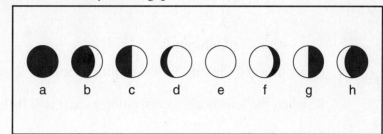

1. Identify the phases of the moon in the figure above by writing the correct term in the space provided.

   a. _____

   b. _____

   c. _____

   d. _____

   e. _____

   f. _____

   g. _____

   h. _____

Answer the following questions in phrases or complete sentences.

2. Why does the same side of the moon always face Earth? _____

   _____

   _____

3. Place the moon and Earth in relation to one another as they would be during a solar and a lunar eclipse.

   Solar eclipse   SUN→   _____   _____

   Lunar eclipse   SUN→   _____   _____

4. Do solar eclipses happen every time the moon travels around Earth? Why or why not?

   _____

   _____

SKILLBUILDER

The moon's diameter is about 3476 kilometers. Earth's diameter is about four times greater than the

moon's diameter. What is the approximate size of Earth's diameter? _____

_____

STUDY GUIDE

19-3   Tides

Match each item in Column I with the most appropriate item in Column II. Write the letter for that item in the blank to the left.

Column I

_____ **1.** tides

_____ **2.** high tide

_____ **3.** low tide

_____ **4.** six

_____ **5.** two

_____ **6.** intertidal zone

_____ **7.** moon

_____ **8.** highest tides

Column II

a. occur when the sun, Earth, and the moon are lined up

b. when the level of the ocean along a coast is at its lowest point

c. the approximate number of hours between high tide and low tide

d. slow-moving water waves with long wavelengths

e. area near shore alternately covered and uncovered by tides

f. affects tides because of its gravitational pull on Earth

g. when the level of the ocean along a coast is at its highest point

h. the number of high tides every day

Place a check mark beside each item that affects tides.

_____ **9.** gravitational forces acting between the sun, the moon, and Earth

_____ **10.** amount of sunlight

_____ **11.** gravitational forces acting on Earth's oceans

_____ **12.** the position of the moon, the sun, and Earth

FIND OUT!

1. How can you figure the difference in height between high tide and low tide on the same day?

_____

_____

2. When is the difference in high tide and low tide greatest? _____

_____

_____